BO Jackson

BO Jackson
PRO SPORTS
SUPERSTAR

Thomas R. Raber

Lerner Publications Company ▪ Minneapolis

LIBRARY OF CONGRESS CATALOGING-IN-PUBLICATION DATA

Raber, Thomas R.
  Bo Jackson, pro sports superstar / Thomas R. Raber.
    p.   cm. — (The Achievers)
  Summary: A biography of Bo Jackson, an athlete who plays
both professional baseball and professional football.
  ISBN 0-8225-0487-1
  1. Jackson, Bo, 1962-   —Juvenile literature. 2. Baseball
players—United States—Biography—Juvenile literature.
3. Football players—United States—Biography—Juvenile
literature. I. Title. II. Series.
GV865.J28R33   1990
796.357′092—dc20
[B]   90-34897
                                                                   CIP
                                                                    AC

Manufactured in the United States of America

International Standard Book Number: 0-8225-0487-1
Library of Congress Catalog Card Number: 90-34897

2   3   4   5   6   7   8   9   10   99   98   97   96   95   94   93   92   91

Contents

1
An All-Star Blast

Bo Jackson stepped to the batter's box looking strong and confident. He whipped his bat through a practice swing. He popped his chewing gum. He steadied his batting helmet on his head and spread his legs into a wide stance.

Bo almost looked like a football player as he got set at the plate. He might have been a running back, coiling into position in the backfield. But Bo Jackson of the Kansas City Royals was preparing to bat in major league baseball's 60th All-Star game. He was the lead-off batter for the American League.

A sellout crowd at Anaheim Stadium in Anaheim, California, buzzed in anticipation. Millions more fans watched on television. Bo's Kansas City teammates knew what they wanted to see.

"Everybody's to the point that they don't want to miss his at bats," Frank White of the Royals said.

"They might see something they've never seen before."

Bo swung at Rick Reuschel's second pitch. It was a sinking fastball, down and inside. Bo connected and sent a towering drive to center field. He hit the ball so high that some fans thought it would not reach the fence. They thought the ball would be caught.

But Eric Davis of the Cincinnati Reds knew better. Davis had hardly moved in center field before he knew the ball was out of the park. All the players in the National League bull pen stood up to get a better look at the ball's flight. It landed 448 feet (134 meters) from home plate in an open area beyond the center-field wall. A group of young fans raced to retrieve the souvenir.

With one swing, Bo had given the American League a run. "I'd heard about his power and strength," Rick Reuschel said. "I saw it firsthand tonight."

National League manager Tommy Lasorda of the Los Angeles Dodgers was just as impressed. "The ball he hit sounded like he hit a golf ball," Lasorda remarked. "That guy is just awesome."

Later in the All-Star game, Bo made a difficult catch of a line drive into left field. He also stroked a base hit and stole a base. With this, he became the second player ever to hit a home run and steal a base in an All-Star game. Willie Mays, the Hall of Fame outfielder for the San Francisco Giants, had been the first.

Bo's All-Star game performance showed that he was in a class with the best, including the great Willie Mays.

Bo showed flaws though, too. He struck out on three pitches in his last trip to the plate. But Bo's all-around effort sparked the American League to a 5-3 victory. He earned the game's Most Valuable Player award and gained new respect from his peers in the rival National League.

"For me, one the the best reasons for coming here was to see what this guy could do," said Tony Gwynn of the San Diego Padres, one of the National League's top hitters. "I'm a believer. He can do everything they say he can. It's scary to see a guy that size, with not an ounce of fat, who can run like the wind, who's got an arm like a cannon."

9

The Kansas City fans love Bo Jackson.

"Bo is phenomenal," said Bo's American League teammate, Kirby Puckett of the Minnesota Twins. "He almost blew out my shoulder when I tried to give him a 'high five' after his home run. I think my shoulder might be separated," Puckett joked.

Bo had shown that his baseball skill is something special. But he is remarkable for another reason. Not only is Bo an all-star slugger—Bo Jackson also plays professional football!

2
A Wild Boar

The Los Angeles Raiders were trapped. They had the ball on their own eight-yard line. A gain of even four or five yards would have looked big. The Raiders decided to try a simple running play. They gave the football to their 6-foot, 2-inch (185-centimeter), 222-pound (100-kilogram) running back, Bo Jackson.

Bo scooted around the left end. The Cincinnati Bengals came rushing forward. A Bengal defensive back had an angle on Bo and looked sure to bring him down.

But Bo turned on the speed that can carry him 40 yards (36 m) in 4.1 seconds. He left the Bengals chasing him all the way to the end zone. It was his second touchdown of this game in November 1989, and it was only the first quarter.

Just four months earlier, Bo Jackson had been astounding his opponents in baseball's All-Star game.

As soon as the baseball season ends, Bo changes uniforms.

Now Bo was leaving football pros gasping for breath.

"There's no question he's a Hall of Fame back," said Clem Daniels, a former rushing leader for the Raiders. "They come along every 20 years, one like him."

Raider corner back Lester Hayes agreed. "Bo is unreal. He's a step beyond stupendous. He was destined to be a football player."

It now seems obvious that Bo was destined to be a football player—and a baseball player, for that matter. But when he was younger, no one was sure what he would become. Some adults, including his mother, thought Bo might wind up in prison.

Bo was born on November 30, 1962, in Bessemer, Alabama, near Birmingham. He was the 8th of his mother's 10 children. Bo's mother, Florence, worked as a housekeeper in a hotel. His father, who did not live with the family, was employed as a steel worker.

Money was scarce. Bo, his mother, and his four brothers and five sisters all lived in a two-bedroom house. At school, Bo received free lunches through a special program.

Yet Bo was full of spirit. His mother named him Vincent Edward Jackson. But by the time Bo was six, his brother and some cousins were calling him "Boar" or "Boar Hog."

"They said I was tough like a wild boar," Bo says. "After a while they cut it short and called me Bo."

Bo's rough nickname was fitting for a guy who often got into trouble. "When I was little, every time someone got beat up, or hit in the head with a rock, or a bike stolen, or a window broken . . . they came looking for me," Bo says. "I was the neighborhood bully."

Bo's mother warned him that he had better straighten up. Sometimes she punished Bo by waking him before dawn. She would make him take out the trash or mow the lawn in the dark.

Bo still made time for sports. But playing well came almost too easily for him. Being a bully seemed like more fun. "I played Little League baseball for about two weeks before they decided I was too rough and moved me up to the Pony League," Bo says. And Bo kept causing trouble.

One summer day when Bo was 14, he and some friends were walking to a swimming hole. On the way, the boys passed a hog pen that belonged to a Baptist minister. "We stopped and threw some rocks," Bo says. "One rock just led to another." In no time, $3,000 worth of pigs were dead. Bo's mother threw up her hands. "My mom told the minister, 'If you want to send him to reform school, go ahead,' " Bo says. "I guess that's when I said to myself, 'I'm gonna have to straighten up.' I realized I could get sent off for some of the stuff I was doing. I just kind of cooled out."

As a youngster, Bo had a speech impediment. Some people mistakenly thought Bo was stupid because of the way he spoke. Even as a young pro, Bo still stuttered mildly sometimes. The speech condition made Bo somewhat shy growing up. But through sports, he found another way to express himself.

Bo set out to be an all-around athlete at McAdory High School in McCalla, Alabama.

At McAdory High, Bo excelled in many track-and-field events, including the pole vault.

"It left me too tired to run with my old friends," Bo says. "Plus I made new friends that didn't get into trouble."

Bo proved outstanding in any sport he tried. By his junior year in high school, Bo was faced with the same questions he would confront later as a pro. Which sport should he play—football, baseball, or track? Which should he devote the most time to?

Bo wanted to play several sports. But his three older brothers told Bo he was foolish. "They said I wouldn't succeed in three sports, that I should stick with one," Bo says. "I told them I was going to do it, that it was none of their business what I did."

So Bo played baseball. He often played shortstop and center field. As a pitcher, he could throw a fastball 92 miles per hour (147 km/h). By the age that most boys are playing baseball in the Pony League, Bo was already playing in a men's semipro league.

Bo ran track. He set four individual state high school records in track and field, as well as the Alabama prep decathlon record. Distance running was the only track-and-field event at which Bo didn't excel.

And Bo played football. As a senior, he earned all-state honors at running back and played defensive end. On offense, he once knocked down three players with one block. But Bo's mother was set against football. She was afraid Bo would be hurt.

Bo also was an excellent swimmer who loved the high dive. Sometimes he would stop by tennis practice and beat the varsity players by just fooling around with a borrowed racket. But there was one sport Bo never cared for—basketball.

One day, Bo was doing his homework in the school gymnasium while the basketball team was practicing. When practice ended, Bo walked onto the court and picked up a basketball. He made sure no one was looking, took a couple of steps, and dunked the ball behind his head. Then he picked up his books and left. Bo just wanted to prove he could do it.

Bo graduated from high school in the spring of 1982 and was offered a contract to play baseball for the New York Yankees. The Yankees offered a lot of money; Bo's family could have used it. But Bo turned the offer down. Instead, Bo wanted to go to college.

Bo could have attended almost any school he chose. He was highly recruited because of his athletic skills. But he wanted to be careful. If he had chosen a "party" school, Bo says, "I would have flunked out my first term." He wanted to get a good education and not be valued for his athletic abilities alone.

While growing up, Bo had dreamed of playing at the University of Alabama under long-time coach Paul "Bear" Bryant. But a recruiter at Alabama said that Bo would not likely be allowed to play until the end of his sophomore year. "Not me," Bo said, "I'm going to play right now."

He decided to attend Auburn University in Auburn, Alabama. He enrolled in the fall of 1982.

College life stopped Bo cold at first. Early in his freshman year, Bo borrowed a friend's car and drove to the bus station, planning to buy a ticket home. He sat in the bus station for six hours thinking. He was lonely and scared. But he thought of how disappointed his family and friends would be if he left school, and he turned around and headed back to campus.

"In college I learned responsibility," Bo says. "Some days you open a book and say, 'I can't do this, I got a headache.' Then the little bell rings in your head and you say, 'I got to.' "

Bo decided to study family and child development at Auburn. His mother originally got him interested in child development. "It always fascinated me how my mother single-handedly raised all of us," Bo explains. "And we never saw stress on her face or where she was tired from raising us."

Bo turned down offers from the New York Yankees baseball club and the University of Alabama football team. He chose instead to play football at Auburn under coach Pat Dye.

18

On the football field, Bo set Auburn career records by rushing for 4,303 yards and 43 touchdowns. In his sophomore year, he led Auburn to the Southeastern Conference championship and a victory in the Sugar Bowl. He was named the Most Valuable Player in the Liberty Bowl as a junior. In 1985, Bo rushed for 1,786 yards and 17 touchdowns and was awarded the Heisman Trophy, college football's highest honor.

Bo also excelled in track in college and was considered one of the nation's premier college baseball players. Through his senior year, he kept fans guessing about what sport he might play as a pro.

"Right now I'm leaning toward football," Bo said in the fall. "Come spring, I'll be leaning toward baseball."

Sometimes he joked about his plans. "I may chuck them both and go fishing."

Most people thought Bo would chose football. After all, he was the Heisman Trophy winner. Surely he would want to test his football skills against the best.

In the spring, Bo was selected by the Tampa Bay Buccaneers of the National Football League. He was the first player selected in the 1986 draft. The Buccaneers offered Bo a rich contract. But Bo didn't budge. Tampa Bay was a poor team with a weak offensive line. Without good blockers, Bo would take a lot of hits in the backfield. He knew an injury could end his career quickly.

During his junior year at Auburn, Bo batted .401 with 17 home runs and 43 RBI.

"In football, you never know which play will be your last," Bo explained. "I couldn't put up with that."

The pro baseball draft came up in June. But Bo was passed over in the early rounds. The baseball teams were sure that he would decide to play football. They didn't want to choose him and waste a draft pick.

But Bo surprised them. When the Kansas City Royals took a chance and chose him in the fourth round, Bo signed a three-year contract.

"My first love is baseball," he said after signing. "I went with what's in my heart."

Everyone expected the 1985 Heisman trophy winner to play pro football.

Bo (left) signed a contract with the Kansas City Royals in 1986.
Many were shocked at his decision.

3

Out in Left Field

After one week as a professional baseball player, Bo Jackson had a batting average of .065. He had struck out 14 times. Bo was playing for the Royals' minor league team, the Memphis Chicks. This was Class AA baseball, two steps below the major leagues.

Some people wondered if even Class AA ball was too advanced for Bo. They thought the Royals should have started him in Class A, or in a rookie league. Others thought Bo was crazy to be playing professional baseball anywhere. He should be playing football, they said.

In football, Bo could have been an instant star. Football players usually go straight from college to the big time. Lots of money and fame can be theirs immediately. They travel by jet and can eat in fine restaurants.

Bo got off to a slow start with the Royals. He began in the minor leagues with a poor batting record. But he soon moved to the majors and won the starting spot in left field.

Baseball players, on the other hand, usually begin their careers in the minor leagues. In the minors, they sharpen their skills, hoping to be called to the majors. Along the way, minor leaguers travel by bus. Some of the rides are long and boring. Players eat budget meals. It's not poverty, but it's not first class.

Bo was used to instant success. He was giving up a lot to learn baseball in the minors. Yet he had confidence in himself, even when he was playing poorly.

At times, thanks to his raw talent, Bo could hit the ball a long way. Bo had never faced professional pitching, though. The pitchers discovered that Bo could be fooled by curveballs and by fastballs high and inside. After 45 at bats, Bo had only four hits and was batting .089. He struck out far too often.

In addition, Bo needed to learn the finer points of baseball. Even as a pro, he didn't really know the proper way to take a lead off first base. But he learned quickly and his play improved. In September 1986, the Royals called Bo to the American League.

In his first major league at bat, Bo scratched out an infield single. He was clocked at 3.62 seconds running to first base, a time that put him among the fastest players in the league.

Bo's first major league home run came a short time later. It was a 475-foot (142-m) blast, the longest at that time in the history of Royals stadium. But Bo went on to strike out 34 times in 25 games with the Royals. He batted just .207 that season.

Some critics said Bo wasn't ready for the majors. They said the Royals were simply afraid to keep Bo in the minors because he might get restless and jump to professional football.

Some questioned Bo's attitude. On occasion, Bo refused to take fielding practice with his teammates. He was a rookie, but sometimes he behaved as if he were an established star.

Some people thought Bo missed playing football. Maybe that's why his play was erratic, they said. But Bo said it wasn't so.

"There's nothing about football that I really miss," he remarked. "I enjoyed every minute of it. I look back and reminisce over it, but I don't miss it. I'm having too much fun for second thoughts."

In the off-season, Bo spent three weeks in Florida getting special coaching. He learned how to hold his glove properly when fielding ground balls. He learned how to get a better jump on fly balls and how to be more patient at the plate.

The Tampa Bay Buccaneers held rights to Bo as a football player for an entire year. They tried to interest him in switching sports. But Bo was all baseball. He came to spring training in 1987 still lacking some skills, but he impressed the Royals' veterans with his new attitude. No one worked harder than Bo.

The Royals planned to assign Bo to a Class AA team at the start of the 1987 season. But Bo said, "I set my goals high. I'm shooting for the top. I only set one goal, and that was to make the team."

Bo not only made the Royals' roster. He won the

starting job in left field. Strikeouts continued to haunt him, however. He fanned five times against the New York Yankees and tied a major league record for strikeouts in a nine-inning game. But Bo bounced back. He had 18 homers and 45 RBI by midseason—both team highs.

Royals veteran Hal McRae was cautious, however. "Bo's not out of the woods yet," McRae warned. "Bo's education is going to take three to five years and will include some rough times."

Rough times came almost immediately. Bo's play faltered after midseason. He lost his starting job in left field. In the last half of the season, he hit only four homers and drove in only eight runs. He batted .235 for the year.

Bo also struck out an alarming 158 times in 396 at bats. He might have set the American League strikeout record, except he hardly played during the last two months of the season.

The Royals fell out of the pennant chase. Many blamed their collapse on an announcement Bo Jackson made on July 11, 1987.

4

Raider Traitor

Two days before the All-Star break, the Kansas City Royals were two games out of first place in the American League Western Division. That's when Bo Jackson stunned his teammates. He announced that he would pursue a career in pro football when the baseball season ended. He would play for the Los Angeles Raiders of the National Football League. Football would be his "hobby," Bo said. He would return to play baseball in the spring.

"My number-one priority is the Kansas City Royals," Bo claimed. "I have to do my job with the Royals before I do anything else. Whatever comes after the baseball season is a hobby—just like hunting and fishing."

Players, coaches, and fans were shocked. After the announcement, Kansas City fans threw small footballs into left field after Bo struck out or made a poor play. They booed him and called him a "Raider Traitor."

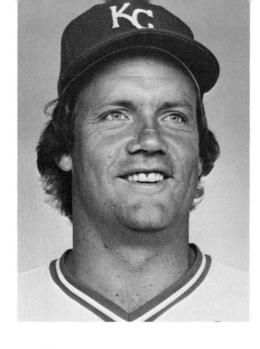

George Brett and his Kansas City teammates were upset when Bo announced he would play football in the off-season.

Bo's teammates were upset too. "I'm mad and the team's mad," outfielder Willie Wilson said.

"It's destroying us," exclaimed Danny Tartabull.

The players were also angry at the Royals' management. They didn't think that the team should allow Bo to play both sports.

Most professional baseball players agree to avoid outside activities that might injure them. A contract might forbid a player from riding a motorcycle, for example, or from climbing a ladder to fix the roof of a house.

"I look at my contract and there's a paragraph two, three inches long which tells me what I can and cannot do," first baseman George Brett remarked. "Now maybe I can go Brahma bull riding or take up sword fighting."

Football people were upset too. They thought Bo was silly to think he could play football as a "hobby." They said Bo might be a target for rough treatment. Some players might be eager to punish him for taking football so lightly.

"Football is the next thing to war," said Jim Brown, former Hall of Fame running back for the Cleveland Browns. "It's no hobby by any means. If he thinks football is like fishing, then . . . he'll be the bait. And if he compares it to hunting, he's got to be the target."

Bo had kicked around the idea of playing football for some time. His obligation to the Tampa Bay Buccaneers had expired after one year. This meant Bo was free to be chosen by another football team in the 1987 draft. The new team would be taking a chance, however. They couldn't be sure that Bo would be willing to switch sports. The Los Angeles Raiders took that chance and drafted Bo in the seventh round in the spring of 1987.

Bo liked the idea of playing for the Raiders *and* the Royals. He thought, "Hey, maybe this isn't so crazy—Bo Jackson suceeding in two sports. I called my lawyer."

"I've been doing both sports since the ninth grade," Bo explained. "It's just the way I wanted to spend my time. It had nothing to do with trying to be the world's greatest athlete. It's just that I'm the type of person who doesn't like too much time on his hands."

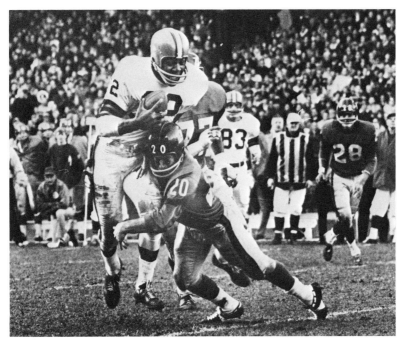

"Football is the next thing to war," said Jim Brown (shown rushing against the New York Giants in the 1960s). Brown knew firsthand what kind of punishment Bo would be in for.

Bo had heard rumors that he didn't play pro football because he was afraid of failing or being hurt. "I wanted to shut some people's mouths," he said.

"I took all the flack, all the criticism, and all the 'He can't do its' and used it to fuel *my* fire," Bo said. "I like competition. It's not the money, or the fame, or the glory. It's the way I breathe."

Bo talked to his teammates on the Royals to help them see his position. "Once they understood I was going to be a baseball player first and a football player only afterward, it was okay," Bo says.

But many questions remained. Was Bo too self-confident to realize how difficult playing two sports would be? Had he forgotten how rough football could be? Could he honestly give his best to both teams? Would he wear himself out?

Despite widespread criticism, Bo was confident. "I know I can do both sports," he boasted. "It's all mental."

Bo followed in the footsteps of Jim Thorpe, another superstar athlete who played baseball and football at the professional level.

Many experts wondered if Bo could ever fulfill his potential in either sport if he tried to play both. Playing at the professional level is a full-time job. In the off-season, a baseball player might learn to switch-hit, for example, or he might improve his base stealing or fielding. But if Bo was playing football, he would not have that chance.

Several professional athletes have been active in two pro sports at once. But few have had distinguished careers, and most did not play football. There is a great risk of injury in football. Most two-sport pros choose less dangerous activities. Dave DeBusschere and Gene Conley, for example, were major league baseball pitchers in the 1960s who also played basketball.

Other players were active in one pro sport and later switched to another. Danny Ainge, for example, played baseball for the Toronto Blue Jays in the 1980s before switching to the Boston Celtics basketball team.

But Bo was most often compared to Jim Thorpe, a star athlete of the early 20th century who played both football and baseball. Thorpe starred in track and field in the 1912 Olympics at Stockholm, Sweden. He went on to become an outstanding pro football player, but was only average in baseball.

Many people thought Bo could play both sports adequately. But could he play both at a superstar level? Still another question remained. How would Bo's football teammates accept him? The regular baseball season isn't over until early October. Pro football starts in August. Bo would be walking into the football season late.

Bo joined the Raiders after the baseball season ended. The Raiders needed help. They usually were play-off contenders, but in 1987, the team had fallen on hard times.

"You make allowances for special people," said Raider coach Tom Flores. "And our players want to win. If he helps us win, they'll cheer him."

Tom Flores, head coach of the Raiders when Bo signed on, wanted a winning football team. He didn't care what Bo did during the off-season.

5

A Point Proved

Bo Jackson pulled a silver-and-black jersey over his head. The number on it was 34. The baseball season was over, and Bo had not worn his blue-and-white number 16 for the Royals in almost five weeks.

Bo was suiting up for the Los Angeles Raiders' game in Seattle against the Seahawks. It was November 30, 1987—Bo's 25th birthday. Bo knew his family would be watching the Monday night game on television.

That autumn had already been eventful for Bo. On September 7, he had married Linda Garrett, a woman he had met in classes at Auburn.

About a month later, Bo got his first chance to play pro football. Bo did not play much in his first four games as a Raider, but he averaged a gain of more than six yards each time he carried the ball. He scored his first NFL touchdown in the fourth game.

Bo blasts past the Denver Bronco defense.

It was an acrobatic 35-yard carry against the Denver Broncos. Bo's teammates were impressed with his skill.

"For the first time in a long time, I got chills down my spine on a football field," said Bo's teammate, defensive end Howie Long.

Bo said he had been "experimenting" in his first four games with the Raiders. But in the game against the Seahawks, Bo was prepared to give his full effort.

The evening started badly for him. He fumbled. Seattle recovered and went on to score a touchdown. But before the game was over, Bo would capture the imagination of everyone watching.

First, he caught a 14-yard touchdown pass. Then he left the Seahawks trailing him on his way to a 91-yard touchdown. It was the eighth-longest run from scrimmage in NFL history. Later Bo scored again—this time on a hard-fought, two-yard run. Bo had to carry big Brian Bosworth of the Seahawks with him into the end zone.

"No excuses," said Bosworth. "He just flat ran me over." Bo rushed for 221 yards that night. It was the 10th-best single-game rushing performance in NFL history. Bo had set Raider records for the longest run from scrimmage and the most yards gained rushing in one game. The Raiders won the game, 37-14, snapping a seven-game losing streak.

The next week, Bo's name was everywhere. He was proving that he could succeed playing two sports. Many sports fans enjoyed watching him prove his point. Others resented his nerve. Bo was getting too much praise, the critics said. He was thinking only of himself. Other top athletes had the talent to play two sports, but they stuck to one.

Two weeks after the Seattle game, Bo returned to Kansas City. The Raiders were playing the Kansas City Chiefs. Arrowhead Stadium was jammed. The Chief fans came to see their hometown team. They also came to see Bo Jackson. Bo was a Raider, of course. But the fans couldn't forget that he had been a Royal all summer.

The publicity for Bo inspired the Chiefs to play their best. "We respect Bo as a great athlete," said Chiefs' defensive end Mike Bell. "But we were getting pretty tired of all the talk about 'Bo this and Bo that' . . . all that talk helped get us fired up."

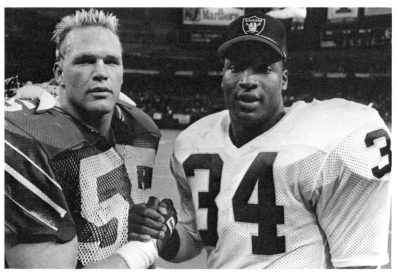

On the field, Bo often butted heads with Brian Bosworth of the Seattle Seahawks. On the sidelines, however, Bo and Brian became good friends.

Jackson in action

The Chiefs beat the Raiders, 16 to 10. Bo played only eight minutes because he hurt his ankle in the first quarter. He gained just one yard on three carries and caught only one pass for four yards. What's more, Bo's injured ankle kept him out of the last two games of the season.

But Bo had proven his point. He could play two pro sports in one year. He could play them well. People would now argue about which sport was his best.

6

One of the Guys

Bo Jackson arrived at spring baseball training a week ahead of schedule in 1988. He put the past football season out of his mind. Bo knew he had something to prove. He had played poorly at the end of the 1987 season. Some experts expected Bo to start the baseball season back in the minors.

But Bo won back his starting position in left field. He missed a month of the season with a hamstring injury, yet he became the first Royal to hit 25 home runs and steal 25 bases (he stole 27) in a season.

Bo still struck out too much. He fanned 146 times. His defense was spotty, too. He made seven errors. The Royals were widely picked to win the American League Western Division. But they finished third, 19½ games out of first place.

Still, Bo finished the season as a solid major leaguer. Maybe he was not yet a superstar. But he had the potential to become one. The fury over Bo's decision to play football was over. The fans no longer booed him. Now when he came to bat they chanted "BO, BO, BO."

Bo was also growing closer to his teammates. "It's what I always wanted," Bo remarked. "I just wanted to be one of the guys. I couldn't be happier right now." Even so, the Royals and the Raiders kept wishing Bo would pick one sport to play. Each team hoped he'd pick theirs.

Ten days after the baseball season ended, Bo joined the Raiders for the 1988 season. As in the year before, Bo arrived long after the rest of the players. He shook hands with old teammates. He met new players. He skimmed the playbook and took a few sprints down the field. Bo Jackson was ready for football.

He played again in front of the Kansas City fans in October. Even more people than the year before turned out at Arrowhead Stadium. They watched Bo rush for 70 yards and a touchdown in a 27-17 victory for the Raiders.

Bo pulled a hamstring in the Raiders' next game, but went on to gain 580 yards and score three touchdowns for the season.

The 1989 baseball season was marked by Bo's big All-Star game. He went on to hit 32 homers, knock in 105 runs, and steal 26 bases that year—despite missing 27 games because of a leg injury.

Bo sometimes struggles with strikeouts. But when he connects, watch out!

Bo still battled with strikeouts. He fanned 172 times; 14 more times than anyone else in the majors. In May, Bo struck out six straight times against the Texas Rangers' ace pitcher, Nolan Ryan. In Bo's next appearance against Ryan, the Texas fireballer smoked a fastball close to Bo's head. But Bo came back and cracked a 461-foot (138-m) home run into the center field bleachers. It was the longest home run ever hit at Arlington Stadium.

Bo's teammates continued to warm up to him. Soon, they fully accepted him playing two sports. "I was upset . . . and I said some unfortunate things," remarked Willie Wilson about his first response to Bo's announcement. "But I've come to learn, Bo's such a good guy, I just admire him."

Bo became more and more popular with the team. On hot summer days, long before game time, Bo would entertain his teammates by trying to cook an egg on the stadium turf.

Sometimes in practice, Bo would stand next to the batting cage pretending to use his bat as a rifle. He would take "aim" and pretend to shoot fly balls out of the air.

The others players loved to watch Bo bat. They traded stories about the long drives they had seen him hit. They talked about the times he batted left-handed in practice just for fun and hit long drives just the same.

Bo's teammates still teased him about acting like a football player. Baseball players are usually quiet and calm before their games, but Bo would get fired up the way football players do. "Let's go. Let's go," he would cheer. "We've got a game to win."

Bo knows polka dots.

Some baseball players receive special coaching or just relax
during the off-season. But Bo has another game on his mind.

Bo enjoyed another successful football season in 1989. He gained 159 yards on 13 carries against the Bengals in November. And his 92-yard run in that game, coupled with his 91-yard burst against Seattle the year before, made him the only runner in NFL history to record more than one rush of more than 90 yards. For the '89 season, Bo gained 950 yards rushing.

The Royals made a poor showing in 1990, but the team's off year didn't seem to affect Bo's game. He hit three home runs in three trips to the plate on July 17 before a shoulder injury sidelined him for more than a month. But Bo bounced back. On his first at bat after his injury, he smacked a record-tying, fourth consecutive home run.

Yet the question remained. Now that Bo had shown he could play two sports, why didn't he concentrate on one?

"I know I can do both sports," Bo responded. "There's nothing physical about it. It's all mental. For me, the athletic part of both sports comes easily. If I can handle it in my mind, everything else comes easily."

7

Not an Ordinary Person

What kind of person is Bo Jackson? People who first meet Bo often notice the unusual way he talks. Bo sometimes refers to himself as "Bo" instead of "me" or "I." "Bo is going to do what's best for Bo," he might say.

It is no surprise that Bo likes to keep busy. "Idle time is something that doesn't fit into my agenda," he explains. "I don't get tired until I'm not doing anything."

Bo likes to spend most of his free time at home with his family. Bo and Linda have two sons, Garrett and Nicholas, and a daughter, Morgan. During the baseball season, the Jacksons live in a five-bedroom house in Leawood, Kansas, a suburb of Kansas City. During the football season, they rent a condominium in the Los Angeles area. Bo and Linda both share in the grocery shopping and house-hold chores.

Bo arrives at the 1984 Sugar Bowl ready to rock and roll.

52

"The smartest thing I've ever done was to get married and start a family," Bo says. "When I leave the ballpark, I leave everything there. When I hit the driveway, I become a husband and father."

Bo has a number of hobbies. He likes archery; some days he'll come to the stadium with a bow and arrows. He'll set up a target underneath the stands and shoot bull's-eye after bull's-eye, to the amazement of his teammates. Sometimes Bo fishes and hunts animals with a bow and arrow.

Bo likes music, especially gospel records. Al Green and Mahalia Jackson are two of his favorite singers.

Relaxing at home with Garrett, 1987

For the athlete who doesn't like too much extra time on his hands, two sports are better than one.

Friends from college say that Bo was a lousy dancer. They were surprised that such a good athlete couldn't dance very well. Bo also likes airplanes and automobiles and drives a Ferrari Testarossa.

Bo almost never works out in his free time. To keep in shape during the two months between the football season and spring baseball training, Bo says, "I take walks in the woods with my wife." Although he can bench press 400 pounds, Bo does not regularly lift weights.

Still, Bo stays in excellent condition. In college he ate a lot of popcorn and potato chips. But his eating habits have improved. On the field, he likes to nibble on sunflower seeds during breaks in the action.

Despite his tight schedule, Bo says he doesn't get tired. He rarely sleeps more than a few hours a night. "On my days off, I'm up at 7:30 making myself do something to stay busy," Bo says. "At 2:30 in the afternoon, I'm wishing I was at the ballpark."

Bo often does charity work. He especially likes to work with young people. He advises them to study, avoid drugs, and try to contribute to their communities. He is a regular visitor to children's hospitals.

On the street, Bo will stop and help if he sees people having car trouble. He'll wait with those in need until an ambulance or the police arrive. "Even if it was my worst enemy I'd stop and help," Bo says. "I just do what I think is right."

In January 1990, Bo went back to school at Auburn. He was just a few classes short of a degree in family and child development. Bo wanted to be the first in his family to get a degree from a major college. He hoped it would inspire his younger relatives to do the same. When his professional sports days are over, Bo hopes to have a career working with kids.

Bo visits with June Henton, the dean of Human Sciences at Auburn University. In January 1990, Bo returned to Auburn to finish his degree.

In February 1990, Bo signed a multimillion-dollar baseball contract. It was less money than he had asked for, but Bo was not disappointed. "I'm not in this game to get all the money I can," he says. "I don't want to be known as a guy who cares about all that, a guy who carries a pocketful of money. I'm not that type of person."

Nevertheless, Bo makes plenty of extra money from endorsements. Some days, his lawyer receives as many as 25 offers from companies that hope Bo will help advertise their products. Bo's most well-known endorsement was a commercial he made for Nike athletic shoes. The commercial was first shown during broadcasts of the 1989 All-Star game. Bo's performance, both in the game and in the commercial, brought him acclaim from millions of fans.

The ad showed Bo playing an assortment of sports. Meanwhile, other professional sports stars talked about his skill.

"Bo knows baseball," said Kirk Gibson of the Los Angeles Dodgers.

"Bo knows football," added Jim Everett of the Los Angeles Rams.

"Bo knows basketball, too," said Michael Jordan of the Chicago Bulls.

Did Bo know about hockey?

"No," said Wayne Gretzky of the Los Angeles Kings.

Bo jams with rock and roll great, Bo Diddley.

The commercial ended with Bo showing that he was not very good at playing the guitar. Rock and roll Hall-of-Famer Bo Diddley told Bo, "Bo, you don't know *diddley!*"

Of all his accomplishments, Bo is most proud of being his own person—in charge of his own life. He likes being known for his self-discipline and self-assurance. He may never compile the lifetime statistics of an athlete who excels at one sport, but he will know he has made his own decisions about his career.

"No one will live my life for me," Bo says. "There's going to be a time when I'm going to give up a sport. I know that. But right now, I feel I have the ability to display talents in both sports and I'm going to do that. I really don't know if anyone is having a better time than I'm having now. I feel like I'm sitting on top of the world."

How does Bo manage to do it all? "I'm not an ordinary person," he explains.

BO JACKSON
Auburn University statistics

FOOTBALL
Rushing

YEAR	GAMES	ATTEMPTS	YARDS	AVERAGE	TOUCHDOWNS
1982	11	127	829	6.5	9
1983	11	158	1213	7.7	12
1984	6	87	475	5.5	5
1985	11	278	1786	6.4	17
Totals	**39**	**650**	**4303**	**6.5**	**43**

Pass Receiving

YEAR	PASSES CAUGHT	YARDS	AVERAGE	TOUCHDOWNS
1982	5	64	12.8	0
1983	13	73	5.6	2
1984	4	62	15.5	0
1985	4	73	18.3	0
Totals	**26**	**272**	**13.0**	**2**

BASEBALL

YEAR	GAMES	AT-BATS	RUNS	HITS	AVERAGE	HOME RUNS	RBI
1983	26	68	14	19	.279	4	13
1985	42	147	55	59	.401	17	43
1986	21	69	21	17	.246	7	14
Totals	**89**	**284**	**90**	**95**	**.308**	**28**	**70**

60

American League statistics
Kansas City Royals

YEAR	GAMES	AT-BATS	RUNS	HITS	AVERAGE	HOME RUNS	RBI
1986	25	82	9	17	.207	2	9
1987	116	396	46	93	.235	22	53
1988	124	439	63	108	.246	25	68
1989	135	515	86	132	.256	32	105
1990	111	405	74	110	.272	28	78

NFL statistics
Los Angeles Raiders

Rushing

YEAR	GAMES	ATTEMPTS	YARDS	AVERAGE	TOUCHDOWNS
1987	7	81	554	6.8	4
1988	10	136	580	4.3	3
1989	11	173	950	5.5	4

Pass Receiving

YEAR	PASSES CAUGHT	YARDS	AVERAGE	TOUCHDOWNS
1987	16	136	8.5	2
1988	9	79	8.8	0
1989	9	65	7.7	0

ACKNOWLEDGMENTS

Photographs are reproduced through the courtesy of: Los Angeles Raiders, pp. 1, 12, 28, 33, 36, 38, 40, 41, 42, 48, 54 (top), 63; Kansas City Royals, pp. 2, 6, 10, 22, 24, 30, 45, 54 (bottom), 61; San Francisco Giants, p. 9; Birmingham News Company, p. 15; Auburn University, pp. 18, 20, 21, 47, 52, 56, 64; Pro Football Hall of Fame, p. 32; Independent Picture Service, p. 34; Bill Sumner, pp. 50, 58; Kenneth Jarecke, Contact Press Images, p. 53. Front cover photographs: Los Angeles Raiders (top), Kansas City Royals (bottom). Back cover photograph: Bill Sumner.

64